Bidisha is a writer, broadcaster, film-maker and artist. She specialises in human rights, social justice, gender and the arts, and offers political analysis, arts critique and cultural diplomacy tying these interests together. She writes for the main UK broadsheets and presents and commentates for BBC TV and radio, Channel 4 News and Sky News. Her most recent book, *Asylum and Exile: The Hidden Voices of London*, is based on her outreach work in UK prisons, refugee charities and detention centres. Her first film, *An Impossible Poison*, has been highly acclaimed and selected for numerous international film festivals.

THE FUTURE OF SERIOUS ART

Bidisha

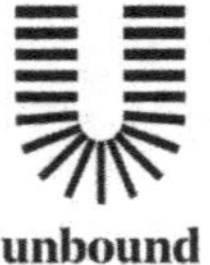

unbound

First published in 2020

Unbound
Level 1, Devonshire House, One Mayfair Place, London W1J 8AJ
www.unbound.com

With the kind permission of Tortoise Media

Text design by Ellipsis, Glasgow

A CIP record for this book is available from the British Library

ISBN 978-1-80018-009-3 (paperback)
ISBN 978-1-80018-017-8 (ebook)

Printed in Great Britain by CPI Group (UK)

1 3 5 7 9 8 6 4 2

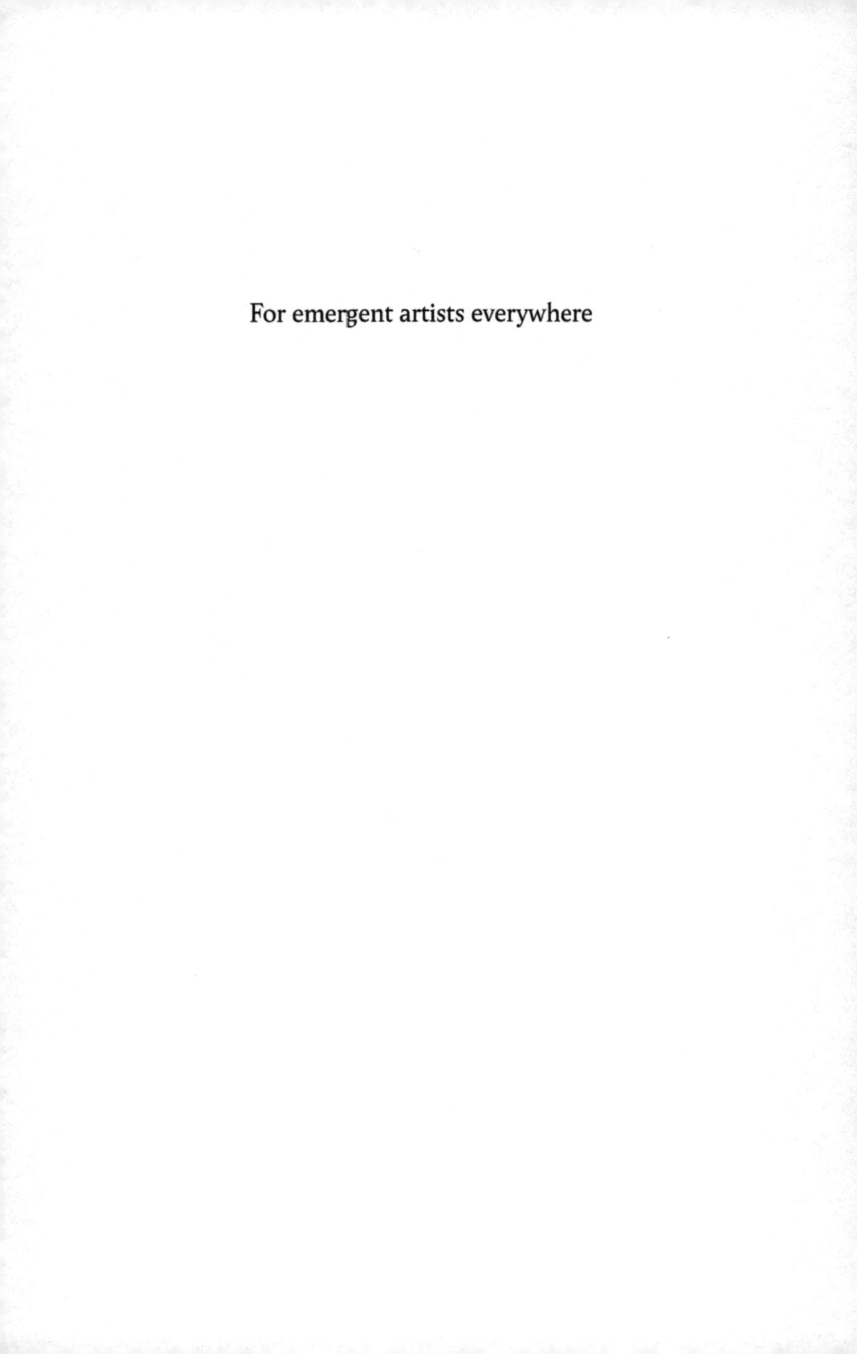

For emergent artists everywhere

FOREWORD

Where and who do we want to be?

How might we get there?

What might happen if we stay on our current course?

This is one of the five books that, together, comprise the first set of FUTURES essays. Each short book in the set presents a beautifully written, original future vision by an accomplished writer and subject expert. Read individually, we hope these essays will inform, entertain and challenge. Together, we hope they will inspire readers to imagine what might lie ahead, to figure out how they might like the future to look, and think about how, collectively, we might make the transition from here to there, from now to then.

Over the life of the series we aim to publish a diverse range of voices, covering as broad a view of the future as possible. We ask our authors to write in a spirit of pragmatic hope, and with a commitment to map out potential future landscapes, highlighting both beauties and dangers. We are hugely proud of each of the essays individually, and of the set overall. We hope you get as much out of reading – and arguing with – them as we have from the process of getting them out into the world.

This first set of FUTURES would have been impossible to publish without the enthusiastic support of Tortoise Media, Unbound and the subscribers whose names you'll find listed at the back of each essay. Michael Kowalski, Tortoise's Head of Product, introduced co-founder Katie Vanneck-Smith to the idea, and she made it happen. Annabel Shepherd-Barron's unparalleled strategic capabilities kept the project steady and on course. Matthew d'Ancona offered superb editorial guidance with extraordinary kindness and generosity of spirit, and Jon Hill's designs for the book jackets are elegant perfection. Fiona Lensvelt, DeAndra Lupu and their colleagues at Unbound have proved wonderfully creative and flexible throughout.

This first set of FUTURES essays was commissioned in autumn 2019, in the midst of the Brexit saga, and edited in spring 2020, in lockdown, as Covid-19 changed everything. As we write, it looks unlikely that, by the time you read this, our lives will have settled into any kind of normal – old or new. Still, argument, wit and enlightened thought remain amongst our greatest strengths as a species, and even during an era as stressful and disorienting as the one we are experiencing, imagination, hope and compassion can help us mine greater reserves of resilience than we might expect. We hope these essays can, in a small way, help us find some light at the end of the tunnel.

Professor Max Saunders, Series Editor
Dr Lisa Gee, Programme Director and Editor
May 2020

THE FUTURE OF SERIOUS ART

Every child on the planet is a serious artist. I'm not being glib: if you want to find the serious artists of the future, look at the toddlers and nursery children of today. For a child, there's no difference between learning and creation, between information and imagination, between exuberant play and necessary brain development. It's all part of the same thing and it arises by instinct.

Nobody needs to teach a child how to play. They do it naturally, creating images, stories, songs and movement. This is true even of children who have experienced incredible trauma – be it war and forced displacement or sexual abuse and neglect. Suffering does not stifle the creative drive, even though what it produces might be grim or disturbing. What children have experienced, what they feel emotionally and what they think consciously somehow all get expressed and externalised through their games, stories and creations.

A creative being rises above petty artistic distinctions. Adult artists who feel stymied in their creativity could learn a lot from observing children's creativity. Children do not create unnatural borders between artistic disciplines. They don't regard their drawings as 'visual art', their living room plays as 'theatre', their sketches as 'comedy skits' or their songs as 'music and composition'. Nor do they see themselves as artists working in one field as opposed to another. They do not even consciously choose the art forms they explore. Instead, they unthinkingly adopt whatever appeals in the moment, adapting to it naturally. It is only adults – and, to be honest, often critics and commentators who are not artists themselves – who sneer when a musician wants to act, or a novelist wants to direct, or a visual artist wants to record an album. There seems to be a suspicion of those who are artistically talented in more than one field. I also wonder if in England there might be a certain cussed jealousy and a resentment of success, a desire to knock down and devalue the successful which nurtures this impulse to sneer.

It's amazing how quickly natural creativity gets squashed out of children. It happens when the instinctive creative drive gets broken down into lesson plans and choices about which formal exams to take. It happens when governments don't invest in the arts and humanities across the board: in drama and movement, art, literature, music theory and performance, but also in languages. It happens when exam targets, points and 'key stages' overwhelm a more generalised sense of accomplishment, exploration, culture and depth of character. It happens when you have a teacher who refuses to see your talent or nurture your dreams, when you have a syllabus that is unimaginative. It happens when you are the victim of low expectations and meagre opportunities. A plant that isn't watered dies.

When I was a small kid I was bursting with creativity – as most children are. I wanted to be a designer, and I remember my headmistress's face dropping like a brick when, aged nine or so, I said as much to her. I'm not sure what she thought I meant: a dress designer? A seamstress on the high street? Either way, she was not impressed. Until then, my favourite thing to do was sit at my miniature desk, with my little baby blackboard in the background, and make things out of wooden building blocks, or construct peculiar sculptures out of seemingly rubbish items like broken wicker baskets and squashed drinks cans.

When I was slightly older my room was like a full-on installation, with huge posters of red sports cars, pop and film stars, Japanese prints and delicate metal mobiles competing with my own artwork and piles of art books and fashion magazines and sketchbooks and mugs of paintbrushes and heaps of plastic jewellery. I loved costume and still do. I collected postcards of any artwork that caught my fancy and occasionally I set them all out on my bed and looked at them, for sheer visual pleasure. I didn't know how one artist linked to another or where each of them stood in the history of art.

When we are that age, art appreciation has no borders, no sense of history and no judgements.

I went towards whatever I was drawn to. The radio was always on, I made fake radio shows recorded on cassette with my friend Gemma and I loved watching films. My favourite subject was art. Of course, this is as much a story about privilege as anything else: I enjoyed a comfortable and hugely supportive home life that valued education, culture and self-realisation and provided me with every avenue, both practical and psychological, for growth and exploration. As well as school I did an after-school club every night, including several lots of orchestra and music theory, gym, dance, violin and saxophone classes, art club and dance club. Even in junior school, once a week I performed with the string quintet in morning assembly. It was painful to get older and have to let some of these activities go, to choose some things above others. You lose sides of yourself when you do that.

But, then, I was given plenty of opportunity to pick up skills and explore my talents (or lack thereof) in the first place. A born and bred leafy north Londoner, I came of age solidly within the nineties heyday of Tony Blair, New Labour, Cool Britannia, the Young British Artists, fashion mavens, Britpop and exotic continental discoveries like pesto. I began my career in 1993, when I was fourteen and fifteen, covering the arts for a range of style magazines including *i-D* and

Dazed & Confused, and signed my first book deal with Harper-Collins at sixteen. I've never worked for free.

As unusual as all this may seem from the vantage point of the leaner 2020s, a career trajectory of this sort was very much in keeping with the times. There was a great deal of optimism around, integral as it was to the New Labour project: rebranding the ambition and drive of the yuppie Thatcherite era into something more artsy, more global. Capitalism, but with a lower-case c. Art itself became co-opted into capitalism, with organisational funding, government investment and institutional support. It was part of the 'cultural sector', the 'creative industries'. There was nothing wrong with becoming rich and famous in the New Labour era – as long as there was a design element, an artsy element, a lifestyle element, a bit of *Ab Fab* style and swagger. Even things which were not traditionally regarded as being part of the cultural scene – running a bar and making cocktails, owning a restaurant and being a chef, designing big buildings – got swept up in the momentum. Before you knew it, the Met Bar's mixologists (a chilling precursor of the 2010s baristas, only with booze), architects like Richard Rogers and Zaha Hadid, industrial designers like Thomas Heatherwick and chefs and restaurateurs like Marco Pierre White and Raymond Blanc were stars.

Behind the decadence and hype, however, there was some substance. It was a glamorous, fast and deeply creative era, with a lot happening in art, film, fashion, design and architecture. Most of the artists I witnessed emerging then as glam young rebels now have fully established international careers and continue to develop: from Tracey Emin, Zadie Smith, PJ Harvey, Björk, Junya Watanabe, Rei Kawakubo, Hussein Chalayan, Richard Billingham and Sam Taylor-Johnson to Wolfgang Tillmans, Lars von Trier and Sofia Coppola. Photographer Corinne Day, fashion designers Sophia Kokosalaki and Alexander McQueen and stylist Isabella Blow are tragically no longer with us. There was a feeling then that anything was possible, including making a living as an artist or even as a journalist writing about the arts.

If you look only at that one decade of the 1990s, it would be easy to dismiss what was happening as a transient 'scene', an explosion of coke and glitter and nothing more. But mere scenes dissolve into nothingness. This one didn't. Most of the people who began their careers then have flourished and gone on to create significant bodies of work, without repeating themselves, rehashing old themes or growing stale. They were not just bright young things, bullshitting by day and partying by night.

I won't deny that the champagne and various other things flowed like mother's milk during that era. But its cultural output started in a burst of youthful exhilaration and has matured and deepened appropriately since then. The artists who emerged at that time were, and are, serious about what they do. Life has a way of weeding out the fakers eventually.

As a rule of thumb, serious art will always be dismissed at first. It will be seen as cheap, as trashy, as empty, as uneducated and insufficiently dutiful to the artistic influences of the past. It will be maligned for its decadence or, alternatively, for its crude populism. It might be damned with faint praise in the moment, but not honoured as being of lasting value.

When artists come along who are so fresh that they kick over the traces of the past and usher in a new era, the old guard, sensing a threat to their money and power and networks, instinctively react with fear and hostility. The stalwarts of the past know in their bones that something new has arrived. The new creators of serious art will be derided as grifters or social climbers. Their work will be mocked – because mocking something is a way of tempering fear. If you're in search of serious art in the future, listen for the sound of scornful laughter.

When I look at the young of today – the tweens and teenagers of 2020 – I am at once hopeful and angry. Angry because I think young people deserve the support of their schools, their after-school clubs, the art spaces and rehearsal rooms, drama schools and dance schools, the civic spaces and street corners, the off-syllabus projects and weekend lessons that will support their creativity. I want to see investment going into these enterprises so the next generations of artists are supported. I want to see a pipeline of talent from first beginnings to industry heights, a pipeline that covers all classes, all ages and all regions and rewards talent with grants, opportunities, jobs, commissions and career development so the talented ten-year-old kid can pursue a lifelong creative career in whatever areas they want.

I'm hopeful because I see that even without these forms of direct and material support, young people are doing it all anyway. What I love about teenagers today is that they possess much of the DIY philosophy, the unbridled creativity and the multidisciplinary approach that characterised not the nineties but the eighties. Austerity Britain in the 2020s has many parallels with the early years of Thatcher: the sense of limitation, of an unsupported society where it's easy to fall down between the cracks, the stalled social mobility and the breakdown in civic trust.

But there is also an incredible can-do spirit. Witness the forming of countless unofficial (and often unfunded) networks and collectives, guerrilla-style art projects, pop-up galleries and restaurants, fashion shows, illustration projects, dance performances, short films and photographs, Instagram poetry, short-term partnerships and deliberately undefined group projects. The light-footedness and openness to experimentation and collaboration, without corporate sponsorship or institutional frameworks, is a hallmark of the punk and

New Romantic eras and a welcome recombining of different art forms.

On the one hand, the ad hoc nature of the emergent generation's approach allies it with street art, with the clandestine, the rebellious and the spontaneous, with graffiti artists and disruptors. At the same time, it is extremely avant-garde in its experimentalism and bravery, its ability to turn anything and everything into art and to combine apparently disparate disciplines into one project. The creators might be as cool as you like to look at, but they are all children at heart. And that's a huge compliment.

That said, there are big differences between being interested in art, wanting to create and aspiring to forge a long career as a professional artist. Each stage presents challenges and, as ever in life, talent is not enough. This is true whether you want to be a musician, a director, a choreographer, a novelist, a playwright, a fine artist or a designer. The principle is the same: you need strategic shrewdness, social skills and intuitive abilities, professionalism, good instincts, good contacts, political nous, determination, a fine balance of staying power and flexibility and (of course) a peppering of good luck and good timing. Success only happens when all those factors converge. The fact that emergent generations might be creating their work digitally and releasing it online doesn't change this. They may gain instant exposure and make great contacts, but the real-world challenges of making an income, making a living from that income and forging a long-term career remain the same.

So much comes down to background: being supported and encouraged. Having the emotional and financial investment from all quarters: family, school, pastoral care, access to after-school clubs and inspiring venues in the town or city around you. And there has to be a broader culture, a mainstream culture of access and appreciation. At least art galleries are still free to enter, as I believe they absolutely should be. Slowly, major theatres, dance venues and emergent-theatre spaces are staggering the prices of their tickets to make them more affordable.

The fact remains that we are at a precarious tipping point when it comes to encouraging talent and taking it from its raw state to the world stage, so that gifted people actually become names. Students who enter university to study the arts may well rack up a great deal of debt by the time they are twenty-one, with no guarantee that they'll be able to get a job and pay it off quickly. London, where the overwhelming majority of all cultural organisations is based, has become extremely expensive to live in – prohibitively so for those who want to buy their own homes but do not have family money.

Some of the problem is structural. The arts sectors themselves – all of them – are splintered and informal, project based, freelancer heavy, mutable, interconnected and lacking in strict definition. Of course, this gives an enjoyable sense of freedom and variety. A little touch of chaos is always inspiring and it is a fun challenge in itself to carve out a career and navigate a path in such an environment. This is why so many artists become obsessed with 'making it'; it is not just about gaining recognition for good work well done. It's also about winning the game. But that same environment is not transparent, meritocratic or governed by reliable and fair rules. There's no pension and no grievance process. The earnings are low for all but a tiny minority. Success, when it comes, is often brief.

Such a system is intrinsically hostile to anyone who needs to make regular money to live, who is blessed with talent but who finds strategising cheap and unpleasant, who is not already stacked with advantages and social capital and a sense of entitlement.

I take comfort regarding the future from looking at the past. It's easy to recall bright spots in world history – everything from the heyday of Constantinople to Renaissance Florence to the Swinging Sixties – when art and money, political power and cultural influence, fame and glamour collided. But those were just bright spots, a lucky concatenation of opportunity and invention. It doesn't mean the societies that produced them were equal, or just, or inclusive, or open-minded. Serious art has always had a risky, dangerous existence. 'Pure' artists – those who don't do anything except make their art – are vanishingly rare and always have been. Those who did survive in the past did so by patronage, sponsorship, official appointment. They did it by courting or being adopted by their social superiors, in heavily class-bound societies that operated along feudal conventions. For all its defects, today's cultural scene is at least an improvement on the artistic environments of the past, from which women artists of any class, men of lower classes and most foreigners of any sex or class were locked out.

So when I predict that serious art will be encouraged in the future, remember that there were many centuries before us when serious art was not encouraged at all, except for the very gifted and the very few (who were also well-connected white men). This has never stopped artists creating, even if they did it in secret. In all of this, the most tragic thing to me is the artist who stops creating, through lack of encouragement and loss of heart.

Paradoxically, the terrible thing about the current economy is also the excellent thing about it. We are in a race to the bottom when it comes to wages, with the proliferation of zero-hours contracts and the normalisation of the gig economy. The bottom has dropped out of the old wage structure and social mobility has ground to a halt. However, *purely from an artistic standpoint*, ground zero, the absolute bottom, is at least a firm springboard from which to create.

When I speak to creative youngsters (those between the ages of ten and twenty) I am struck by their practicality and optimism. It is older generations, in particular those who lived through economic boom times and years of cultural growth, who are disillusioned and pessimistic. Today's young people don't expect to make any money from their art. Yet they haven't lost their ambition. Instead of forging one career they often have a job, sometimes but not invariably in a creative field. They run entire parallel artistic careers with no loss of energy, focus and drive. They also apply creativity and artistic thinking to other areas of life: to anti-sexist and anti-racist activism and political engagement, to questioning the rules of the world around them, to their living conditions and the family-like friends they gather around them and to their leisure activities.

This approach may well set them in good stead for the future. After decades in which the government has obsessively insisted upon the importance of science, technology, engineering and maths, the march of automation may well force a radical rethink of priorities.

I predict that there will be a revolution in the way artists are seen. This will happen increasingly as globalisation breeds homogeneity in the great cities and conurbations across the world. Governments will realise that what makes each of their respective countries unique is the talent of its residents, their originality, their creativity and their ability to make new things that thrill us and make us think.

This is a very separate question to the algorithms, metrics and billion-dollar calculations of the entertainment industry. Art has value – and that value may not be reducible to words, or quantifiable, or 'provable' in any narrow statistical sense. Indeed, box-ticking and 'learning outcomes' – so much a part of the spirit of the age – are quite at odds with the spirit of art.

As machines colonise more and more of what humans do, there will be a reassessment of what it is that artists offer, what makes them unique and important. There may come a realisation that they are much more than 'content providers' supplying the last-minute colour and wit and gloss on the surface of things. As the years pass, there will be a recognition that artists, with their counter-intuitive talent for survival, natural ability to create something out of nothing, to reflect and reflect upon what is happening in the world today, are in fact custodians of some of the most valuable riches in the nation. One artist's output is not replaceable by another, it is not replicable by a machine and it has a powerful capacity to bring people together. In the future, serious art will be recognised as a serious asset.

One question which has always bedevilled artists has been massively exacerbated by the digital revolution – which, in truth, has only just begun. It is the question of exposure. I was lucky to begin my career during a time of economic prosperity and high investment in publishing, film, art, fashion and the media. It was before the 2008 recession, before the War on Terror, before the bottom dropped out of the advertising market, before the technological transformation of everything and well before the rise of streaming services and tech giants.

Something I benefited from hugely as an artist was this: *my serious art was seen.* It was marketed and made visible. There were the major broadsheets, the red-top tabloids, arts periodicals and women's magazines, the smallish number of TV channels, the handful of 'quality' arts shows on the radio. There were advertising posters, bookshops, interviews and events. I did them all, backed up by the power of proper PR and a proper publishing house – and, of course, by luck and by the spirit of the times. I was not burdened by any particular sense that my early books were coming out at the same time as, and competing for attention with, countless other books, albums, films, TV shows, performances and exhibitions. I did not have the sense that I was fighting to be heard. And, of course, not a single person in the audience had a phone to play with during my events.

This doesn't mean there weren't other barriers – expectations, stereotypes, assumptions – or that success isn't always a popularity contest. But essentially the news about my work was funnelled to the right people in the right ways, in a focused and concerted manner, by people whose job it was. After that I could only hope the project would succeed.

That world has gone. These days, artists must not only create but also promote their work actively, utilising their networks and hoofing and gigging and lugging their stuff up and down both the geographical country and the infinite wastes of cyberspace – all in the hope of gaining notice. They must be marketers, PRs for themselves, community builders, experts in brand development, activists and spokespeople, constant hustlers. Sometimes this works. Often, it feels like it's working when you're doing it, but it doesn't result in sales or significant profile-raising in the long term.

There was a time when advertising led to sales pretty directly. Or, as one publisher said to me, 'Look. If you put a stack of books next to the till, people'll buy them.' This is no longer the case, thanks to the sheer proliferation of information, images, exposure and advertising out there. Every year, the publishing industry puts out more books than we would be able to read in several lifetimes. The same way we look around our homes and feel that we've reached 'peak stuff', we look at our to-read piles, our Netflix queues, all those TV shows and black-and-white films and sitcoms and music videos that have now been digitised and put online and make us feel warm and nostalgic. All that music we've listened to over our formative years and can now hear again for free. Plus all porn and all shopping.

I'm not going to make the lazy claim that the Internet is rotting our brains. But we are certainly living in an age of abundance and overload, with little breathing space between entertainment new and old, between news and commentary, action and reaction. We feel overwhelmed, with good reason.

True, it could plausibly be said that we're living in an age when we have greater access to serious art than ever before. But it's important to be precise about what that means, and what digital experience leaves to those who want to apprehend art in real life. Perhaps it'll be only those things which are unique and impossible to replicate anywhere else: the atmosphere of an art exhibition, say, or a dance performance. Clicking on pictures of paintings or watching the footage from a contemporary ballet isn't the same as absorbing the vibe in situ.

In the future, serious visual art may become even more rare and special than it already is. It will contain details too fine to be captured online. It will have a boutique, handmade feel and be produced in limited editions, or be so large that no photograph can quite do it justice; it needs to be experienced in person, for an immersive effect. The most serious art must be something that can't be endlessly photocopied by the Internet. There will be a return to making, to craft and to the pleasures of ink and paper. This is already happening in publishing.

In visual art, one can also detect a backlash against art that 'works' on sites like Instagram. There is the perennial issue of plagiarism and copying. These days I direct films and make photographic stills, but I rarely put the stills online. I don't want them to be endlessly ripped and re-ripped across the Net, or tagged in other people's tweets. I produce actual items people can own, in limited editions of fifty or so, and I keep them physically small, like precious keepsakes or votive objects. They have a sheen and texture, a weight and holdability that I can't convey in a snap, and don't want to.

But artists are also reacting against the way 'online' makes them think. The drive for surface approval, for likes and comments and retweets, warps the way you approach art-making. The tactile joy of the process is lost. The connection to intuition and natural flow is dialled down. Instead it becomes an attention-seeking exercise, a calculation. You start thinking about the colours that will pop in digital, the compositions that will look good in thumbnail size. Even if it does get you what you want – a momentary hitch in the infinite online timespace Moebius strip – it doesn't actually get you anywhere. You don't sell the piece, you don't gain gallery representation, you don't get funded to produce further work. You were just a blip in a stranger's entertainment stream. It's like producing cheap clothes that have hanger appeal but sizzle like cheap polyester the moment you get close and touch them.

I predict that instead of getting cheaper in the future, serious art will become even more detailed, delicate and sumptuous. It will break out of the square or rectangular format and the smooth gloss sheen and become textured, stippled, immersive, even degradable.

I was talking to a curator recently. She wanted to create a sculpture park in an area of the world that is gloriously beautiful but extremely humid. Instead of great rusting sculptures, I pitched her an idea I've wanted to explore for a long time. I love soft sculpture, its tactility and melancholy, its sinister cartoonishness, and I'm interested in traditionally feminine crafts: all the intricately skilled and beautiful work women did for centuries only to have their skills taken for granted, devalued and mocked. Embroidery, needlepoint, papercuts, knitting and sewing. I wanted to make a series of rag dolls from the packs you can still buy in old, 1960s-style haberdashery shops, dolls of girls and women in all different colours and outfits, and leave them to rot steadily in the sculpture garden. Possibly I would return every three months to photograph the decay.

It would be an image of all those news headlines you see about women's murdered and raped bodies being found in the woods. It would be about female fear and pain, about the forensics and fetishisation of the discarded female form in crime shows. But it would also be an image of the small woman, the woman who has traditionally been a belittled outsider in the macho world of monumental sculpture. It might be documented online, but the full melancholy and creepiness, the anger and fear and pain, would only be communicated fully if people underwent the experience of travelling to the sculpture park itself.

Perhaps, instead of us all shouting to be heard, the future of serious art is actually one of greater integrity and modesty than before. We will create, and hope that people find our creations. If not, we will have to make do with the joy of the process, the pleasure of the means rather than the ends.

When it comes to TV, music and film I think the changes will be in a different direction. There are occasional returns to limited-edition cassettes or special vinyl releases for specific projects, which have charm and novelty value and their own cohorts of dedicated fans. But, generally speaking, digitisation has so fully infused these three areas that we will never go back to the norm of having a big box TV, a stack system, CDs and enormous speakers. Instead we will rifle through seemingly infinite lists spanning all ages, all genres, all formats. Albums, TV series and films alike will get longer and shorter. They will shrink to individual episodes or expand to odysseys of film immersion. They will reward a half-hour's attention or a full lost weekend. Do I think that's good for one's mental and physical health? Nope. But I think it's artistically interesting. The Internet is infinite and it enables all manner of experimentation and indulgence.

In a strange way the TV, film and music versions of the experimental prog-rock album, the space opera, the mind-bending LSD trip and thought experiments are all back again. Authorship, style and content are all up for grabs. Some of the things which are most derided today seem like works of conceptual genius to me: people reviewing chicken shops or opening boxes of make-up on YouTube; others filming themselves playing computer games or eating meals; people cutting their own hair or posting their vegan 'journey'. In a weird way, it's total genius. But, to move up a step from that, so many of the comedians and performers who never felt able to send a pitch to the BBC in the hope of it being read, or who didn't have the contacts to make that step in the first place, are crafting music, making films, performing sketches or devising dance that they're putting online – which are fantastic. One thing the digital revolution has proved indubitably is that there is talent everywhere, from all people, in all places, at all levels of society. It is only encouragement and opportunity which fail people, not some deficit in their own gifts.

This doesn't mean that everyone's a winner in the digital revolution. It's easier than ever before to create, but harder than ever before to gain notice or make a career. All the people putting their work online are creating it at some cost. Not just in terms of energy and time expended but often at a financial cost as well. They will make no money from what they do, yet they risk their work being plagiarised and appropriated as 'inspiration' by more powerful cultural players. This has already happened in the fashion industry, with young, unknown illustrators' motifs being copied wholesale by major high-street retailers for prints on clothing and accessories like cute enamel pins. When the young artists tried to launch a legal claim against the (very famous) clothing brands, the brands ignored them or intimidated them through viciously expensive legal threats.

The technological revolution has not, as some hoped, yielded a digital utopia when it comes to the redistribution of money and power. Instead it has led to the consolidation of power by tech giants and mega-content mega-creators like Netflix, Hulu, Disney, Facebook, Amazon, YouTube and Google. Some are entertainment companies. Some are entertainment companies that are also online shops. Some are entertainment companies that are also search engines. Some started off as nothing more than video-sharing sites and online contacts books but now make films, TV, sketch shows, podcasts and live broadcasts. Soon they will be funding their own investigative journalists and producing news reports. We're witnessing the consolidation of political, commercial and cultural power, and it's worth billions. It's also American, not British. Britain takes on board so much of American news and entertainment that it's easy to forget the relationship doesn't go both ways and the absorption is not mutual.

There's plenty I could say about that and about the coming fascist tide, climate apocalypse and World War Three, but this is an essay about serious art and I promised I'd be positive and constructive. There is an argument to be made that, despite the sheer jaw-dropping hierarchical power of these tech companies, they might positively influence the kind of artistic output the rest of the world receives. They could, if they wanted, make it more diverse, more global, more inclusive in terms of sex and race, perspective and language. They could scout for varied talent and commission widely. They could find new creators, new stories. They could go beyond the stereotyped narratives. That still involves mainly male, mainly white American executives right at the top of each company exercising their power. But given that the customers for their products ('What "product" does Facebook sell?' I ask myself) are unprecedented in their diversity, perhaps business calculation alone, rather than principle, will encourage Big Tech to embrace plurality and inclusiveness. Where morality fails, the algorithms may end up succeeding.

It is easy to forget how spectacularly the world of film and television has changed in a very short space of time. We now inhabit a strange full-immersion state of perpetual entertainment. It feels like a dystopia, it feels like a hellish series of infinite dream sequences and yet... it's good? It's fun? Either way there's a heck of a lot of original new TV and film programming to watch. I think the spirit of serious art will possess film and TV alike and that there will be an erosion of any distinction between genre and the mainstream, between 'high' and 'low' art, between a filmic approach and a televisual approach. TV will come to look like avant-garde absurdist performance art, or like deeply considered arthouse cinema. Film will come with the full-colour thrills and spills of the trashiest comic book, but elevate it into high art. Fashion, film and dance will combine into mini masterpieces that may or may not be adverts, pulling in performers from all fields. Stars of writing and performance will go from home-made clips to having a series commissioned for an online channel, to getting into bed with a mainstream broadcaster, to signing mega-deals for Hollywood franchises.

The entire screen-based entertainment sphere will blend into one thing – content – with one massive caveat. It will all look amazing. The art direction and visuals will be *Vogue*-magazine quality... while *Vogue* itself loses readers for its print version, then goes digital-only, then quietly closes. As soon as one phenomenal TV series that looks like ten lavish feature films tagged together is swallowed down in one gulp it will immediately be forgotten and replaced by something else. But it will be amazing and awesome while it lasts, and the writers, directors and performers on each show will be paid for the project. The question is: how do we get there, to the all-embracing American digital entertainment hell-heaven, from here?

Serious art will still always be lonely, and this is as true of the poet in their ancient garret as the dancer-choreographer putting in eight hours a day of practice or the emergent arthouse director who's been asked to helm ten feature-length episodes for a Netflix series adapted from a bestselling book.

The feeling of success only lasts about five minutes before every serious artist reverts back to who they really are inside. I don't think this will ever change; it's part of human nature. I have witnessed some artists who achieve great renown and find themselves positively transformed by it. Success suits them. They become responsive, practical, energetic, professional. Success seems to give them some missing ingredient, a way of linking their inner creative drive constructively to the outer world, to audiences and allies.

I have witnessed many more people who were spoiled unutterably by success. Who were rattled by the attention and the intrusion, who went mad with ego and vanity. Who junked their family lives thinking their entire existence was going to be given a makeover, only for it to fall flat. Who got spooked and never created anything worthwhile again. Serious art is a rickety, rackety business – and it always has been. There seems to be little predictable relationship between the work that's put in, the talent involved, the atmosphere of the creation of the work, the importance of the work and the effect it has when it is published or released. Success is nihilistic and fame is famously fickle.

Serious art has to be secure enough in itself to ride out all those worldly instabilities. The changeable quality and rapid motion of the outer world is very extreme at the moment. We don't live in steady times and it's hard to predict, writing in 2020, what will happen with galleries, cinemas, bookshops, music venues, music festivals, theatres and performance spaces, even fashion shows and clothing boutiques. Perhaps they will all disappear, replaced by digital experiences shot on a sound-stage and designed to be watched on tiny phone screens. I doubt it, though. Serious art will be deep and communal, as it has always been. People still go to music festivals; they still buy enough tickets to sell out the arts and ideas festivals I speak at. Humans are a social species and will always seek each other out. A feeling communicates itself through a group. That's how we metabolise our impressions and reactions.

Yes, we have to resist phone addiction and passive absorption through those glowing screens. We need to work harder than ever on self-discipline, attention and contemplation. But I don't believe the human race has been permanently ruined. The backlash that's already begun against screen addiction will only grow, and there will be increasing recognition that communal spaces, communally experienced creativity and art are necessary for other parts of human life to function: mental health, a sense of local pride and community, further inspiration for further art. There will be an attempt to reinfuse all of daily life with reality, commonality and connection, and art will be at once the cause, the medium and the beneficiary of this.

That said, the stubborn reality of stalled social mobility, reduced investment in arts organisations, increased authoritarian control of public spaces through surveillance and profiling, and the bleed-out of investment in the provinces and regions (in spite of government rhetoric to the contrary) must be tackled first. Otherwise serious art will be what it has always been: an interest and an occupation of the elite. Something enjoyed almost exclusively by those who have access, money, education, contacts and the leisure time in which to create and contemplate.

If I give the impression that I regard serious art as rarefied and complex, that is because I do think it is – at least, for those who want to go beyond hobbyism and amateurism. It requires a measure of worldly advantage and privilege for those who wish to succeed, and, at an internal level, it requires certain qualities. Self-belief, inner drive, discipline, personal motivation despite an indifferent reception. Having an artistic talent is like having a secret friend, a secret resource, a hidden recourse. As an artist, I am never lonely because my creative self is always with me. But I need to be alone to work and an artist needs to make their creativity their priority. These characteristics go against what is commonly expected of people, and particularly women, in society. We are supposed to go out and work and labour, join and enable, be part of something which is not ourselves: a family and a workplace. How dare we be arrogant enough to make a stand for ourselves as artists?

But there's another much-overlooked element to serious art that I want to touch upon. It's the role of pain and failure, rejection and trauma, isolation and anonymity. These are the things that nurture art just as much as vision and inspiration. They are often the dark matter that fuels much creativity, consciously or not. That desire to explain, to be understood and seen.

We live in an age when two opposite forces are at work. On the one hand, art has become big and bold – whether it's TV and film projects with millions of dollars behind them; or commissions by star architects to create instantly Instagrammable pavilions; or phenomenal book series that are made into massive film franchises. Art looks lucrative, something easy to absorb into globalised capitalism, driven by the market. At the same time, however, the conversation around mental health and unhappiness, anxiety and social pressure is opening up. Young people are leading a sharp critique of the images of perfection, wealth and success we see all around us. They are talking about their truth and their reality, their fragility, their struggles. They are questioning why the world of serious art looks the way it does. They have a truly intersectional way of looking at the world around them, a sense of power, its distribution and where it is absent.

Whether it is in the art world or book publishing, the ballet scene or contemporary theatre, people are noticing who pulls the levers and who does the work. Who is not in the room? Who isn't being heard? Which stories are being told and which are overlooked? Who gets the money and opportunities and who is still broke? Why is it easy for some people and hard for others? These are all difficult and necessary questions.

White supremacy, male domination, racist and colonial attitudes, stereotyping, racist bullying, exclusion, sexual abuse and labour exploitation in the various creative sectors must be examined, or the future of serious art will look depressingly like its past. In this respect, I am cautiously optimistic. There is a real desire for change which will only continue in the future as we question and push at the structures of the world around us.

This questioning process is really about integrity and trust. The increase in many people's mistrust of institutions and authority figures, self-proclaimed leaders and figureheads – so harmful in its encouragement of brainless political populism – is not necessarily a bad thing when it comes to art. Creation itself may be pure, but as soon as it goes out into the world it encounters worldly structures and worldly sins. No single sector in the world is free of inequality, abuse, prejudice and misogyny. No single sector has clean hands and a clear conscience.

In the future – actually, in the near future, since it's already started to happen – there will be a reckoning as institutions and organisations are critiqued and held to account. Whether or not they will change immediately is another matter. After all, they already have immense power and money and prestige and do not need to change, or even to question themselves. At the moment their responses are defensive and enraging. Power does not want to confront itself or go on a learning journey. But with enough pressure, over enough time, with enough disruption and demonstration and unrest, it will have to listen. These febrile times are an opportunity as well as a crisis. In the breakdown of the current order, artists can – with luck – remake the world as they want to see it, instead of beating themselves against doors that are never going to open.

Now that creativity is increasingly infused with political activism and with social questioning, I wonder if there will be any need for critics in the future. Anyone with Internet access can now advertise their thoughts on any art form, cultural product, politician or meal. These thoughts can be raw and unfiltered, considered and thoughtful, true or false, wildly damaging or sweatily reverential. Today's digital culture vultures can write long essays on their favourite films, or can angrily denounce a director for not featuring their favourite character for long enough. They can keep an online journal of their books, advertise their reading progress and boost lesser-known authors. They work in a multi-disciplinary fashion, their essays interpolated with images, video links and access to further archives.

In the long time I've been working, I've witnessed the death of style and fashion magazines, the reduction of space given to arts coverage in broadsheet newspapers and the rise of digitised market-led research which lets galleries, streaming giants and venues log exactly who is showing up for which events and shows, how long they're staying, what they're buying tickets to afterwards and much else. This is quite different from individual artists wanting to know how one critic in particular engages with their work. The digital revolution has enabled everyone to find out what everyone else thinks about everything, effectively in real time. Critics and traditional coverage are not driving people to any particular product. That power has been radically dispersed.

This is a shame because reviewing is an art in itself, as well as being a pleasure to do. It opens up a space for peaceful and lengthy analysis, contemplative engagement and context-setting. Long, fair but critical reviews are always interesting both to read and to create. But they haven't disappeared. They have moved online and are being produced by amateurs, or by others – curators, producers, academics, students – who operate in the same milieu as the media. Leaving aside the question of fake news – the web can weaponise lies about culture, like anything else – a lot of the critically engaged 'fan' or connoisseur critical writing I've read online has been thoughtful and useful. It is politically engaged, analytical and often points me to artists and art histories I hadn't known about. But this high-quality writing is produced for free and it is read for free. The critical establishment has been drained of funding, like almost everything else that digital technology touches.

There are a few websites, funded by wealthy patrons, that are attempting to bring the art of long-form writing, of slow critical consideration and upscale production values, into the online world. The content they host is often beautifully written and elegantly designed. Collections of essays, long-form investigative journalism and creative non-fiction are being published again. But at the end of the day these boutique platforms are massively dwarfed by the sheer word count of immediate action and reaction, gallery selfies and quick takes. Slow connoisseurship is simply not what the overwhelming majority of people are doing.

Sadly, I think the decline of criticism should be viewed with resignation by people old enough to have lived through the heyday of magazines and luxury publications, the BBC's high-quality output and the broadsheets with their lovely, glossy bundles of Sunday supplements that grow ever thinner and sadder and more passé-looking each week.

By all means, if the money is available let us shore up the critical community. But accepting a change in the way creativity is communicated and reflected upon, however painful in the short term, is healthier. We are only in the earliest throes of the digital revolution and it's important not to get on our high horse and cling to the past.

Now that the ways in which art is being considered are changing, I wonder if the places in which serious art is produced will also change. For the past few years I have done outreach work in UK prisons and with charities for ex-offenders, as well as working with mental health charities and resource centres for refugees and asylum seekers. I have seen incredible talent there, both literary and visual. I've been saddened that – simply because of the ways the world works – it is unlikely that any one of the talented amateur artists I've met will 'make it' or be recognised in anything other than a tokenistic, patronising way. For the most part, gallery representation, publisher and agent services, film production or theatre performance deals will not be available to them. Wrong background, wrong colour, wrong age, wrong sex, wrong class, wrong language, wrong manner, wrong approach. This is deeply unfair and also deeply banal: the brute fact that, as much as ever, it's who you know. Does your face fit? Are you clubbable? Are you 'their' sort of person?

That's the status quo. But it is not as secure as it once was. We are at a tipping point when it comes to questions of belonging. The outsider artists are knocking to get in. There is a great drive among arts lovers in all fields to bring the margins to the centre, to root through the periphery and examine who has been pushed out there and why. There is a hunger to find – or re-find – those artists who are old but still working and creating and ask why they never got their dues, or why they received them briefly and were then erased and forgotten, casually written out of official history. There is an increasing drive to look at these official histories – the canon of literature, the lists of cinematic greats, the art history syllabus – and see them for what they really are: profoundly political expressions of power and privilege, lionisation and exclusion. They are values manuals, advertising the time they were created in. They don't tell us anything about art. They tell us something about society. They can change and they should change.

The art that women make and the things we are interested in as artists, what we say and how we say it. The art that people of colour make and the truths we have continually to reassert in the face of resistance, denialism and fragility. The art that second-generation Britons want to make despite constant demands that we talk about race and identity and homeland and belonging and non-belonging and our parents' or even grandparents' 'immigrant experience'. All these things are pushing away at the canon, exerting great pressure from the outside in. Soon, the tiny, little, mainly white, mainly male canon of 'greats' will break, and all the millions of voices it kept out will ooze all over them and drown them out.

For centuries, the work of anyone outside of a bare handful of countries in Europe was not considered serious art. The literature, the images, the movement and theatre and spectacle, the avant-garde explorations and intricately composed music. All of it was glanced at and dismissed for hundreds of years by racist, greedy, arrogant, rapacious colonisers' eyes. They stole it for their houses and museums, and to amuse their guests, but at the same time as coveting it they did not value it. It was seen as primitive, tribal, superstitious, unskilled, instinctive rather than thought through, spontaneous rather than planned, innocent rather than self-aware. It was seen as testimony, exorcism, traumatic suffering, invocation, fetish. But not serious art.

Western institutions will eventually have to confront the reality of Western colonisation and slave-driving. Serious art will remain stuck until they do. But confronting the crimes and violations of the past is relatively easy compared with what must happen in the future: changing. Opening up, breaking down, opening the doors. Letting other people in. Relinquishing power, giving the microphone to other voices and humbly listening and learning. Being quiet and receptive and respectful. Acknowledging not privilege but ignorance. There is a glaring mismatch between all the lovely things people in the arts sectors say about inclusion and diversity, equality and opportunity, building bridges and tearing down walls, and what they actually look like, what they actually do and who they actually give money and support to. If you look behind the camera, tour the gallery's office, visit the publisher's editorial floor or sit in on the board meeting of the seemingly cutting-edge theatre, it will be glaringly obvious who's in the room and who isn't.

Artists have been vocal about this for several decades now. The pain of the excluded, the artists whose ambition was met with condescension and derision, has never been quiet. But these voices of outrage are now much more plentiful and – thanks to the connectivity of the online world – collective, unified and supported. They are part of the age we live in, which is one of revived protest and unmasked outrage at various forms of inequality and power-holding. There are now generations of Britons of colour who love all art forms but inevitably reach a point of radicalisation around race and colour, sexuality and identity, sex and class, and begin to ask questions of the gatekeepers. There will come a time soon when they can no longer pretend that we are invisible, that they can't hear us or see us, or that what we have to say is irrelevant or naïve.

The spirits of serious art and street-level protest will fuse as real-world issues such as these prove too pressing to be ignored. Creative contemplation and activist rage will somehow combine. Increasingly, questions will be asked about why our most revered arts institutions continue to be blind to the sufferings, desires and challenges of millions. Even mainstream forms of creativity – say, superhero films – will take on and reflect these issues, in however fictionalised a form. I welcome this, not only as a necessary corrective but also as a way of dusting the earnestness off capital-I 'Issues-based' work. In the past, issues-based work was often dismissed as worthy, as dutiful and good for you but unpleasant, unenjoyable and separate from serious art or real art or high art.

That distinction is no longer meaningful. We live in an age in which global crises – experienced by many millions of people – have become the addictive and compelling (and awful) narratives that form our everyday experience, just as dramatic as any novel or TV series.

Indeed, in the last few years I've often wondered why I should bother with narrative art at all. Why do I write and direct films when even a cursory look at the headlines far supersedes anything I could make up, for thrills or disasters or absurdity or sheer abject spectacle? The big stories of our time are social stories, political stories, human stories. There is no division between any one of those descriptors. Terrorism and dogma, zealotry and fanaticism, invasion and war, the refugee crisis, acceptance and belonging, race and racism, male sexual violence, machismo and patriarchy, class and privilege, surveillance and control, policing and authoritarianism. Climate change. Serious artists would have to be living in a sealed room not to notice what's happening in the world and how extreme and urgent it all is. Increasingly, I believe, art will take on if not the literal narratives of news reports, then the themes, the agonised energy, the exposure of inequality, the spirit of rage and panic (and even of hope and determination) which are so powerfully emergent these days.

There will be a boldness, bravery and nakedness to the art of the future that will be impressive. In the past, such art may have occupied an underground, avant-garde or niche space. It might have been categorised as protest art or feared as incendiary and insurgent and distributed through guerrilla channels by artist-outsiders or by reactive creators who didn't necessarily see themselves as fine artists. But these issues are now so dominant and unavoidable that these radical considerations will be given mainstream platforms: the major theatres and performance spaces, publishers, galleries and film studios will have no option but to take them on and put them front and centre. There will be a recognition that there's no time left for cultural output limited to escapism or dreamy denial about the world and its future. Humanity's vision will open up to huge and terrible realities, to monolithic, terrifying concerns, to the yearning for confrontation and escape alike. My position is one of weirdly optimistic doom-mongering: serious art will take on big themes and strong concepts because the world is ending in burning and violence.

And on a much less eschatological note, I do think serious art will survive the threat of phone addiction. It would be ridiculous, as well as tragic, if centuries of world culture were collapsed into and lost to a small device. I don't think we should surrender that much cultural power to phones. Yes, my heart does sink when I look down the Tube carriage and people are all staring at their phones with their mouths slightly open. It's even worse when I see someone watching a beautifully shot, written and acted film or TV episode on their tiny screen. At least they're watching it, I tell myself. It's this or nothing, I tell myself.

Serious artists have always bemoaned the philistinism of the masses. That is a constant. It certainly feels that we live in a far more self-righteously ignorant, defiantly troglodyte, insular, uninterested and thuggish culture than before – but that's just a feeling. All the people currently staring at their phones weren't studying sheet music before the digital revolution. One could argue that globalisation and digitisation have opened up vast archives and endless resources for people looking for serious art.

It's important to resist bitterness. The audiences for contemporary dance, for theatre, for film, for painting and sculpture have not decreased. Ticket sales are not down. Venues tell people to turn off their phones when performances are underway. Yes, it's depressing to see them all lighting back up again in the interval, and it's depressing to see people unable to resist their addiction and firing them up mid-film. But they're young. When I was young I was a much bigger twat than that.

Our brains are massive, complex, always-working organs which are processing and consuming huge amounts of information all the time. They are not going to be permanently damaged and impossible to 'reset'. The current wave of concern around online addiction is a good thing, precisely because it encourages us to consider where we are and where we are heading.

In the future there will be a fight to reclaim contemplation. Without contemplation it is impossible to create serious art and impossible to consider serious art. Contemplation is about creating mental and physical space, in peace but not necessarily in silence. It is this which we have lost from the outer world and from our inner selves. We've lost touch with ourselves, with our thoughts, with our bodies and with nature. We've lost contact with the flux of time and with our own instincts. Without this, we can't create. This loss of mindfulness began long before phones, but has been exacerbated by them. The future of serious art depends on an extension of what is already happening: an instinctive move on the part of ordinary people to recapture the feeling of existing in the world, with nothing pulling or scratching away at our attention.

If we can achieve this, we can wrest back what has been taken from us, and free up our capacity for creativity. My final predictions for serious art suggest two opposing trajectories. One concerns the simple act of creation itself, while the other considers the real world and its challenges.

In terms of pure creativity there will be a beautiful combining of multiple art forms. The creators of today have a wonderfully borderless approach to creativity. What marks them out as artists is not any single discipline they adopt or path they mine, but their willingness to explore, to play, to try out different forms of expression and find whatever works. At the core of every true work of art is a sincere expression that is devoid of cynicism. In the future all the art that we have produced, in any form, will be available to be explored and learned from.

But will they be enabled to have long careers? Will they be supported financially and professionally, so that the emergent artists of the 2020s will then craft bodies of work which develop throughout the subsequent decades? Will they have to live through a world war and climate breakdown and end up painting marvellous murals on the inside of their survival bunkers?

As it is, in the UK at least, many foundation courses, training programmes, talent-scouting endeavours, emergent talent initiatives and other ventures enabling professionalisation are not truly democratic, although they claim to be. For a start, you can only go to university if you can afford it – afford the fees, afford the debt, afford the rent, afford the years you'll spend afterwards finding your feet.

Serious art will only thrive if the non-artistic elements of our future world change. By this I mean the unglamorous, unbeautiful issues around location, class, race and sex. I am writing at a time when borders are closing down and insularity is on the increase; when there is a backlash against multilingualism and multiculturalism. In my fantasy, artists of talent can travel and explore, can feed their souls by living, loving and learning (and working) all over the world, with many different people and in many different languages. That may not happen, and it would be a tragedy.

In considering the future of serious art, I am torn between looking at the world as it's most likely to be and looking at it as it could and should be. As it would be, if I were queen. There is much to be heartened by, if we look at the future artists of today, at the kids who are now in their earliest years at school. They will not inherit the jadedness of previous generations. They are engaged, punchy, inventive and realistic. They bring creativity to everything they do. But they are inheriting a world which is divided, unequal, angry and increasingly unstable. I believe we are on the brink of global changes – political, social, cultural, economic and environmental – which will either destroy our future or save it. The world of the future would be nothing without serious art, just as the past twenty centuries would have been nothing without it.

AFTERWORD

In 1924, inspired by a sensational essay they had published the previous year, the publishers Kegan Paul launched a series of small, elegant books called To-Day and To-Morrow. The founding essay was *Daedalus; or, Science and the Future*, and its author, the biologist J. B. S. Haldane, made several striking predictions: genetic modification, wind power, artificial food. But the idea that captured the imagination of his contemporaries was what he called 'ectogenesis' – the gestation of embryos in artificial wombs. Haldane's friend Aldous Huxley included it in his novel *Brave New World*, in which humans are cloned and mass-produced in 'Hatcheries' (it was Haldane who later gave us the word 'clone'). Fast-forward almost a century, and scientists have now trialled ectogenesis on sheep and are exploring its potential for saving dangerously premature babies.

Haldane took no prisoners as he hurtled through the ages and all the major sciences, weighing up what was still to be done. Perhaps because it was his discipline, he was convinced that the next exciting scientific discoveries would be made not in physics but in biology. So, his Daedalus is not the familiar pioneer of flight but the first genetic engineer – the designer of the contraption that enabled King Minos's wife to mate with a bull and produce the Minotaur. Predictions have an unstable afterlife; their truth changes with the world, and while Haldane was brilliant on – and made a major contribution to – genetics, he was sceptical about the possibility of nuclear power. In the wake of the Second World War, and the realities of atom bombs, hydrogen bombs and nuclear power stations, his view of the sciences appeared wide of the mark. Later, when the Human Genome Project became news, he emerged as a prophet again. But while biotech certainly still preoccupies us two decades on, it is the computer that we see ushering in the definitive transformations of the age: artificial intelligence, machine learning, blockchain. And, remarkably, the computer is the one major modern development that not only Haldane but all the To-Day and To-Morrow writers missed.

By 1931, when the series was wound up, it ran to 110 books. They covered many of the subjects that mattered most at the time, from the future of marriage to the future of war, the future of art to the future of the British Empire. Most of To-Day and To-morrow's contributors were progressive, rationalist and intelligent, in favour of a World State and sceptical of eugenics. They wrote well, and were sometimes very funny, and the essays on the future of clothes and the future of nonsense in particular are wonderfully eccentric. And, of course, Haldane wasn't the only visionary. Many of the other writers contributed equally far-sighted ideas: Dora Russell suggested something akin to universal basic income for mothers; J. D. Bernal imagined wirelessly networked cyborgs – a cross between social media and the Internet of things; while Vera Brittain waxed confident about the enshrinement of women's rights in law.

What really stands out now is how, on the whole, the authors seemed to feel freer to be imaginative about the future than our contemporaries tend to be when they make predictions. There seems to be something about the long-form essay that freed the To-Day and To-morrow authors to see further ahead than a short journalistic piece could. Pursuing the logic of an individual vision, while also responding to what others projected, led them to dive deep into their topics in ways that are hard for the more tightly collaborative think-tank approaches of today to replicate. They were also more constructive than most of our contemporary future-thinkers. Of course we'd be mad not to worry about the climate crisis, the mass displacement of people(s), the risks of AI, new diseases (I'm writing this at the height – *maybe* – of COVID-19), asteroid collision and other apocalyptic scenarios. But if we're not only to survive these but also to thrive, we need to think beyond them as well as about them.

We are now almost a century on from the launch of To-Day and Tomorrow, and it feels like the right time to try this thought experiment again. So, for this first set of FUTURES, we have assembled a diverse group of brilliant writers with provocative ideas and visions. The point is not so much to prophesy as to generate new ideas about possibilities that could help us realise a future we might want to inhabit. To-Day and To-Morrow launched visions that helped create the modern world. The challenges we face now are, obviously, different from those of the 1920s and 30s. But our aspirations for FUTURES are the same. We want to change the conversation about what lies ahead so we can better imagine, understand and articulate the new worlds we might want to create.

Professor Max Saunders, March 2020

Max Saunders's Imagined Futures: Writing, Science, and Modernity in the To-Day and To-Morrow Book Series, 1923–31 *was published by Oxford University Press in 2019.*

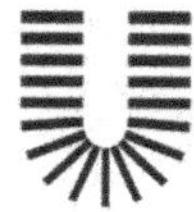

Unbound is the world's first crowdfunding publisher, established in 2011.

We believe that wonderful things can happen when you clear a path for people who share a passion. That's why we've built a platform that brings together readers and authors to crowdfund books they believe in – and give fresh ideas that don't fit the traditional mould the chance they deserve.

This book is in your hands because readers made it possible. Everyone who pledged their support is listed below. Join them by visiting unbound.com and supporting a book today.

With special thanks to Jo Greenslade and Ark Schools

Caspar Addyman
Kathy Allen
John Attridge
William Ayles
Stuart Banks
David Barker
Stephen Beagrie
Ghassan Bejjani

Sarah Bennett
James Benussi
Steve Bindley
Kate Bird
Ian Blatchford
Su Bonfanti
Ed Bonnell
Stuart Bowdler

John Boxall
Zara Bredin
Catherine Breslin
Fabia Bromovsky
Victoria Bryant
Nicki Burns
Paul David Burns
Imogen Butler

Gemma Hitchens

Maggie Hobbs

Meaghan Hook

Simon Howard

Nick Hubble

Simon Huggins

Jenny Hynd

Maggie Jack

Andy Johnson

Rebecca Jones

Danny Josephs

Tanu Kaskinen

Matthew Keegan

Christopher Kelly

Hilary Kemp

Luke Kemp

Fraser Kerr

Adam Khan

Dan Kieran

Andrew Knight

Christine Knight-
 Maunder

Lauren Knussen

Florian Kogler

Michael Kowalski

Simon Krystman

Nikki Land

Ben Lappin

Lyndsey Lawrence

Benedict Leigh

Fiona Lensvelt

Max Lensvelt

Sonny Leong

Miriam Levitin

Joanne Limburg

Linds

Valerie Lindsay

Ivan Lowe

Brian Lunn

Nicola Lynch

Rob MacAndrew

Andrew
 MacGarvey

Jem Mackay

Innes Macleod

Lewis MacRae

Paul Martin

Chris Matthias

Jenny McCullough

Michael McDowall

John McGowan

Neil McLaren

Adrian Melrose

John Mitchinson

Ronald Mitchinson

Kyna Morgan

Ian Morley

Tony Mulvahil

Robin Mulvihill

Peter Mummery

Tessa Murray

Janet Musgrove

James Nash

Carlo Navato

Kelvin Nel

John New

Sorcha Ní
 Mhaonaigh

Christopher Norris

Tim O'Connor

Mark O'Neill

Brian Padley

Michael Paley

Euan Palmer

Nic Parsons

Jaynesh Patel

Don Paterson

Sumit Paul-
    Choudhury

Matthew Pearson

Pauline Peirce

Nick Petre

Benjamin Poliak

Justin Pollard

Harriet Posner

Samantha Potter

Mark Poulson

Kate Pullinger

Slam Raman

Padraig Reade

Colette Reap

Suzanne Reynolds

John Rice Doyle

Stephen Ross

Charlotte Rump

Stuart Rutherford

Keith Ruttle

Cassedy Ryan

Ruth Sacks

Luke Sanders

Martin Saugnac

Max Saunders

Eleanor Scharer

Daniel
    Schwickerath

Duncan Scovil

Alexander Sehmer

Rossa Shanks

Gillian Shearn

Paul Skinner

Christopher Smith

Jan Smith

Katie Smith

Matthew Spicer

Paul Squires

Wendy Staden

Nicola Stanhope

Keith Stewart

Freddie Stockler

Nick Stringer

Elizabeth Suffling

Gilane Tawadros

Georgette Taylor

Richard Taylor

Bronwen Thomas

Luke Thornton

Lydia Titterington

Sophie Truepenny

Mark Turner

Geoff Underwood

Maarten van den
    Belt

Suzan Vanneck

Danielle Vides

Emma Visick

Gabriel Vogt

Claire Walker

Sir Harold Walker

Suzi Watford

Richard White

John Williams

Ross Williams

Catherine
    Williamson

Philip Wilson

Luke Young

Angelique &
    Stefano Zuppet